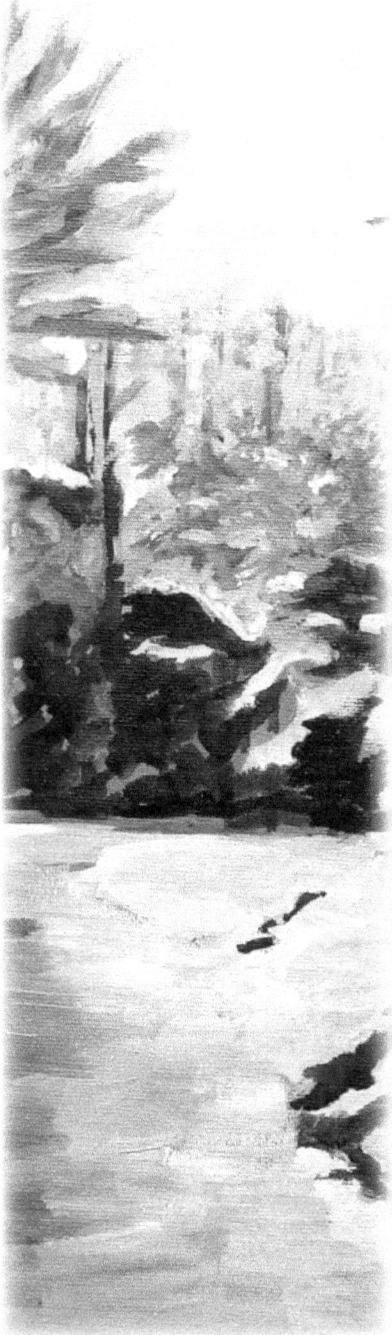

Daily Prayer Lifelines

Saroj Daulat Ram

Published by

2013

To my grandchildren
Anand, Anjali, Monica, Sonia, Anand, Kashia,
Suchin

ISBN 978-1-926926-25-4

All Rights Reserved. Copyright ©Saroj Daulat Ram, 2013.
The author assumes sole rights to the contents of this book.

Cover painting ©Dr. S.V. Anand.

Layout & Design by Shirley Aguinaldo

PRINTED IN CANADA

Introduction

The prayers in this book are mainly conversational and some are confessional. Prayer is our 'lifeline' to God. With deep faith in His omnipresence our spirituality is shaped. Each devotee prays in her own way. The following are some of the ways people connect with God.

1. Conversational Prayer: Here you have a dialogue with your Creator, hoping that He hears you and will answer in His own way someday.

2. Confessional Prayer: Where you admit your faults of omission or commission and ask for His forgiveness.

3. Invocational Prayer: Where you are conscious of a Divine presence and pray in adoration.

4. Intercessory Prayer: Where you pray for the betterment of your fellow man and the world in general.

5. Action Prayer: When you pray while working or walking to help those in need.

6. Petitionary Prayer: When you plead with Him to show you the right path and to lead you there.

Most human beings come in search of God in many ways, but mostly through sad and lonely times you need His guidance or during ups and downs of life. In happy times you give a prayer of thanksgiving for His many blessings and ask for His Divine grace.

Daily prayer is essential to our wellbeing to keep us on the straight and narrow path, to live a righteous life, to obey the commandments, to tell the truth and to be honest with ourselves. These precepts lead to self-realisation which is the beginning of wisdom and ultimately may lead to Nirvana, your salvation. The prayers in this book are my lifelines to God.

Saroj Daulat Ram, 2013

Just Pray

Enlightenment may come
If you pray some
He might hear your cry
If you really try
With a sincere heart
Make praying your part
Pray, reach the skies,
He might hear your cries
Do not give up trying
He is all knowing
He is always listening
Do not shy away
Do not keep Him at bay
Let him into your heart
All you need to do is ask
And it shall be given
Make Him your haven
Pray, pray, ask his help
With Him a bond develop.

Mysterious Are Thy Ways

My Lord let it be stayed
Take me in Thy hand
Let my life stand
As pure as it can
In service of Thee
For answered prayer
One must be a player
Sitting at home
You may pray some
And hope and hope
That God would drop
Fortune at your door
All without get up and go
Work and prayer must go
Hand in hand
In life's musical band.

O Lord of the Universe

Grant me Thy divine grace
So life takes a humane face
Where love and hope prevail
And charity never fails
O Lord, let me never be lazy
This life not be hazy
That I may always do good
That I may always be good
Lord in Thy prayer
I must spend my days
Lord I give thanks for Thy blessings
I bow to Thee in supplication
Allow me to help the needy
In Thy infinite mercy
And those that are destitute
They deserve most fortitude.

Piety is a Spiritual Way of Life

Holiness is its outer garb
In our Creator a firm belief
In doing good play one's part
Follow the Scriptures in daily life
Observe chastity and honesty
And giving of charity
To love mankind
To turn the other cheek
Gentle of speech
In God to believe.

Lord of the World

Lead us by Thy holy light
Away from our darkened plight
Raise our morals to Thy sacred height
Lead us from darkness to light
Grant Thy grace, O eternal guide
Be merciful, O Lord of the light
Pardon our sins in this walk of life
Forgive our trespasses and pride
To Thee our prayers always arise
Fill us with a sense to be wise
Each morning, noon and night
In Thy faith we must abide
O heavenly father let Thy guiding light
Warm the world and keep it bright.

Lord Give Me Faith

That I may never
Doubt Thee ever
That Thou are the beacon
That Thou the heaven
That Thou art my all
This I must recall
That Thou art my soul
Thou art my all
In my heart to hold
Thy love, Thy worship
Is all I ask for
Have me then
In Thy presence
Wherever thou art
Heavenly Father Thou art
Have mercy
Upon all Thy progeny.

Cheer Up

Look up
Look forward
No 'could have'
Or 'should have'
Look ahead
With no regret
Wear a smile
Make it your style
Be right on
At each morn
Bow to the Lord
For blessings you got.

Be My Shepherd, Lord

Guide my life, O Lord
Take me by the hand
And lead me on to stand
Firmly in thy devotion
I am a stranger to Thy notion
Teach me righteous wisdom
Hold my hand and lead me on
I am lost in the ways of the world
Take me on the noble path
Let me be with Thee
On all the days of my life
So I may do some good
Till the day I die

In This World's Long History

Man is alone basically
Utterly lonely
Yet he turns to Thee
In his misery
Thou giveth a silent hearing
Answering prayers a-hoping
Life giver that Thou art
Playing a parental part
Behind the scenes
By heavenly means.
Yet we long to see Thee
Face to face really
The Lord whom I tell my all
Without getting a scold
The quest to see His face
Is a timeless race
To unveil Thy mystery
We need Thy infinite mercy.

Lord, Hear My Pleas

Let Thy wisdom be my guide
Let me live in thy shadow
And make of this life a go.

Bless This World, My Lord

And all those who live in it
Free us of plagues
And other earth aches
Let people be kind
And loving to each other
Free us of exploitation
And of famines and fires
Let there be good harvests
And abundance of food
So no one goes hungry
And have homes that are happy
O Lord have mercy, have mercy
Let all be happy
And have decent family
That adore and worship Thee.

Up and Up You Go

Think big
Go to the top brass
To God no less
Aim high
Reach the sky
Banish the regret
Past to forget
Start afresh
Do not fret
Aim high
Limit is the sky
With His help
You cannot fail
Without it
You will just trail.

Save Me O Lord

That I may act justly
That I show mercy
That I am never lazy
That I walk humbly
Let Thy presence
Be my life's essence
That this my soul
To Thee is bound
Once and for all.

Heavenly Father

Amidst the milling throng
One is really all alone
With one's thoughts
With one's hopes
Only to Thee I whisper a wish
Or a desire my Lord
Only to Thee I open my heart
In a song of lamentation
In a throng I hold Thy hand
As Thy name I chant
And I tell Thee all as to a friend
The two of us one God
And one lost sheep for, Lord,
Even when all alone
Always Thee I call upon.

Om

To Thee I bare my soul
For Thou art my all
The final court of appeal
For my soul to heal
To Thee I bring my joys and sorrows
In hopes of sunnier tomorrows
My requests are sung as prayers
Thou the architect of my affairs
To Thee I bare my soul
For Thou art my all
Hear my call
O master of us all
Come to my rescue
To Thee I am true
Be my guide
Thou art my pride
My master, my guide
O hear my prayers
I beg for Thy cares
To Thee I bare my soul
For Thou art my all.

Om

There are doubts that arise, my Lord
Is there a god that hears our song
Is there a heavenly being in reality
Who will show us mercy
I sure hope so
I want to believe so
For without His presence
Our lives are one empty expanse
Full of sorrows more than joys
Full of empty long senseless days
Without prayers of entreaty
For His everlasting mercy
Life seems like that of an orphan
Like the body missing an organ
He is the parent for all our lives
From infancy to final goodbyes
In His presence we can laugh or cry
Till the day we die
Lord, this is eternal hope
That thou shall us tightly hold
Till finally to Thee we come across.

Om Thanksgiving

I thank Thee, O Lord
For Thy blessings all
I thank Thee for the joys of friendship
For the good family relationships
I bow to Thee for Thy mercy
And I beg Thee for future that is bright
For my descendants and the like
Who follow the path that is right
And Lord, let there be peace on earth
And goodwill to the nations of the world
We beseech Thee to keep us in Thy fold
In Thy loving grip to hold
Never from righteousness to stray
And to walk with Thee on righteous way
Lord be our mentor and our protector
Lord from truth never to falter
Lord have mercy, have mercy
On all and sundry.

In This House of God

I have come to surrender my all
Here have I come to seek Thee
And to find the secret of Thy mystery
Here in this silence is Thy eternity
It is filled with Thy glory
And with Thy bountiful mercy
Here will I find the peace
Here perchance Thy grace
Here will I beg with a beggar's bowl
For Thy mercy for all
Here in the silence of the house of God
In the adoration of the song
Will I find the heart of Thy soul
And reach Thee to become whole.

Divine Grace

Why beg for Divine grace?
Deserve thou the same?
Reveal to me Lord the ways
To achieve Thy Divine grace
Me thinks these are the ways:
Kindness and compassion
Honesty and charity
Work for suffering humanity
Without rewards any
Asceticism and piety
Love of lonely study
Love for all humanity
And above all charity
To all and sundry.

Hold My Soul in Thy Hand

Let it not frizz and frazzle
For I am lost
Looking for a refuge
In Thy haloed house
Hold me close
O my everlasting Lord
Weak and lazy that I am
I ask forgiveness in Thy name
Lead me Lord, lead me on
I am lost and far from home
Show me the way, Thy way
Thy abode so far away
I am lost
Hold me close
Am far from home
To Thee I want to come home.

We Need God

For the quiet talk
To lay at his door
Our ups and downs
To find answers
Through a quiet dialogue
To carry us over
The valley of despair
We usually forget God
When it is time to share
Those ups of success
But it is then the time
To do thanksgiving
For the blessings
As answer to the prayers.

Dear Lord

I send Thee many missives
I wonder if Thou does receive
All my begging notes
My heartfelt calls
O great, great Creator
Where art Thou?
I long to Thee behold
I await Thy call
I beg for Thy grace
Turn away not Thy face
From the sinner in disgrace
Allow me in Thy presence
So I may behold Thy glory
To unfold Thy mystery
Have mercy, my Lord
Have mercy upon this sinner of old.

Lord Here I Am

Dashing off another letter
For when I miss talking to Thee
My day seems to be empty
As if I have left out an important chore
Having not paid my homage at Thy door
As if I have not lived at all
On the day I neglected to call
And knelt at Thy shrine
And I bowed to my Lord Divine
My Lord Thou art the Father
Thou art the universal Mother
Thou the be all and the end all
Of our lives and Thy creation all
Forgive me my Lord for addressing Thee
As friend to a friend so familiarly
Because I run to Thee
With all my misery
I regard Thee as a kith and kin
And not some stranger and foreigner
When I err, when I flounder, and cause hurt
It is I who cry, and hurt
Lord, Thou art my counsellor, Thou art my guru
Thou art my saviour, Thou my God true
Lord, hold me and never let me go
Lord, save me from falling through
Lord, have mercy, have mercy
That is all I ask of Thee.

Om

There is only one longing in the heart
To witness God's effulgence in all its part
To see Him face to face
Before I end my days
To witness His glory
In the Creation story
Lord where art Thou?
Who art Thou?
Unravel Thy mystery, Lord
And take us in Thy fold
Hear us chanting Thy name
Hear our worship for Thy grace
Without this homage
Empty is the life and strange
That we never have seen Thee in person
Or art Thou just an illusion?
All the same, we chant Thy name
In worship and homage
As we bow for Thy infinite grace
As we long to see Thy face.

Thou O Supreme Lord

The source of blissful existence
The source of our intelligence
The giver of our abundance
May we prove worthy of Thy choice
May we hear Thy Divine voice
And follow Thee in righteousness
O Lord, guide us on a path of holiness
O Lord, like a speck of dust
I am being buffeted
Heal, heal, O Lord
Be not too far, O Lord
Hold Anita's hand and help her through
The birth of her child, please do
This is my ardent prayer
This is my fervent cry
O save us, O Lord today
As we to Thee pray
With all our heart and soul
With all our fervour of soul
Help, help, Anand, please.

Thy Temple

Thy house of worship is full of devotees
Singing hymns in Thy praise
In reverence they join their hands
And kneel down in pious stance
They are here to spiritually connect
And find their higher self
And Thou art present they say
Wherever five people gather to pray
And they find their solace
They find their peace
As the sing songs of adoration
As they chant hymns of lamentation
They ask for mercy, they ask for grace
They ask for strength
To go through their days
They are there to renew their faith
They are there to find their faith
They are there to be nearer to Thee
They are there to glorify Thee.

O Lord, I Am Here at Thy Shrine

So you may hear this prayer of mine
Please spur my mind
To worship the divine
To always be kind to strangers
And love the lowliest creatures
To never entertain an ill thought
For even the vilest soul
O Lord, fill me with grace
So I am able to hardships face
O Lord, bless the whole world
And keep it in the palm of your hand
And Thy mercy be all grand.

I Have Come To Pay My Homage

In all humility to greet Thee
O my Lord and master visage
I have come to beg for mercy
For me and mine and the world
O omniscient Lord
Help us to live by Thy rules
And to have lofty goals
Let our lives so shine
As Thee our guide
That the world shall delight
With this our blameless life.

Thou Hath Given Me Reason

And sweet are its uses
But in the matter of fate
That only Thou can shape
Goes beyond reason
It is then we run to Thee
To say why O why me
It is then we supplicate
And beg for mercy
It is then we ask for grace
It is then we long to be
In the comfort of Thy grace
In the warmth of Thy embrace
It is then we look for Thy hand
To lead us from darkness to light.

My Lord, We Thank Thee

Mysterious are Thy ways
Thou may not give for what one prays
The answer comes in other ways
It may be the honours one receives
Or in academic excellence one succeeds
It may be houseful of good progeny
Who honestly do their duty
It may be blessings of good health
Or a sudden windfall of wealth
For Thy many blessings we thank Thee
We beg Thy mercy, O Lord have mercy
Lead us to the righteous path
Forgive us for our trespass
Lead us to be charitable to all
Especially to those who need it most.

My Lord God

Have pity on my soul
Make me whole
Raise me from this dark hole
Of social withdrawal
I am a recluse
To nobody any use
I live in my own world
Please help me, Lord
Make me whole
For Thou art my all
Take my hand
Lead me to Thy holy land
Show me the way
To where they pray
And together they stay
When they pray
In desperation I seek Thee
On my knees I beseech Thee
Come to my aid
Brighten my days
O Master Supreme
Lead me to paradise
Where Thy angels smile
On the great and small
Creatures Thine all
Have mercy upon my soul
O master of us all.

Let There Be Light

O Creator of all life
Let Thy beacon show the way
To eternal life
To the city of light
Where only the angels dwell
Where Thy mercy prevails
Where humanity has a sway
Under Thy guidance
I am trailing downstream
In the murky waters of life
Save me my Lord
Do not close Thy door
Hear my knock
For I am a lost soul
Knocking again and again
At Thy door
Searching for Thy holy form
For without Thee I am forlorn
Knowing not where to turn
So help me God
My saviour, Lord.

In Praise of Thee

O Creator Supreme
Hail to Thee
O Father heavenly
We revere Thee
On bended knee
We beg Thee
For Thy grace
On all our days
We turn to Thee
When in misery
But may we Thee adore
For all our days all
Whether sad or happy
We would adore Thee
For thou art the anchor
Thou the succour
Thou the universal guru
Guide us to pass through
This life in Thy honour.

We honour Thee.

I Pay Thee My Homage

After the day is done
In life's humdrum
Thou art forgotten
But at the first setback
I am back on track
Saying my prayers
Chanting the mantras
Visiting the shrine
Begging for mercy
Saying the rosary
Imbued with piety
Picture of humility
Ego and pride are history
For a while anyway
That Thou have the sway
On my destiny each day
That Thou art
God Thou art.

Lord Almighty

Bless this Thy world
And all its creatures
Great and small
Bless those who err
Be their mentor
And lead them to light
From a darkened plight
Forgive their sins
As they are reborn
Into the holy kingdom
Fill their minds
With thoughts kind
For creatures large and small
Thou art the lifeline
Thou the spiritual prime
Thy mercy giveth the shine
To erring mankind
Crossing safely to Thy side
Will be ultimate ride.

My Prayers Carry No Weight

With the Lord of late
He finds them insincere
They are neither here nor there
For I have made no sacrifice
Is it an answer for a price?
Have made no effort on my part
To deserve His blessing for a start
The promises that I make
Always flounder and break
With what face can I ask the Lord
To answer my prayers for sure
For I have a poor hold
On my weak will all told
All I can beseech my Lord
Please strengthen my resolve
So I am good at times all.

In Thy Enchanted Shrine

Thy presence I come to find
In its tranquil inner sanctum
Away from life's ho hum
I bow to express my reverence
It is here that I find peace
It is here that I seek Thy grace
To witness Thee face to face
It is here that I realize
That Thy wisdom is of the wise
The whole creation is Thy shrine
From valleys to mountainside
That Thou art in my soul
Everywhere all along
Whether in a crowd or alone
For Thou art my soul
Thou, Lord, maketh me whole
Abide with me, Lord.

Lord Help Us

To live a useful life
To make use of our faculties
Help us, help us, help us, O Lord
We need Thee more than ever before
Be our guide in our life
Keep us free of strife
To lead a useful life
Help us, O Lord
We are forlorn
In this world of Thine
Maranatha, maranatha
O Lord come to me, I need Thee
O how I need Thee
Give us Thy solace
Give us Thy word
Help us, O Lord.

In the Deep Silence of Your Being

Love Thy God above all
And pray to the All-seeing
To give you grace above all
To love all humanity
And to see God in each being
That you may gain spirituality
Through love and mercy
For all creatures great and small.

Oh Lord

My prayers are of the begging bowl
I am a mendicant at Thy door
Why do I find it closed
To sinners at Thy door
What must a devotee prove
That he is a lover true
Of Thy glory
Longing for mercy
For Thou art the deity
That I honour most
For I am lost
Amidst the glamour
And the clamour
Of the world
O save me, rescue me, Lord
Without Thee I am lost
For Thou art the host
That I revere most
Have mercy, have mercy
O Lord have mercy
On all and mine and me.

O Lord of Creation

Accept my supplication
With songs of praise
Begging for Thy grace
My Lord, turn Thy holy face
To this sinner in disgrace
Forgive her for promises broken
For going back on her word spoken
To help the needy
After obtaining her medical degree
She abandoned her motherland
And practiced her art in a rich land
She got paid for her services
And forgot all about promises
To help the suffering
In her native land
Lord, forgive her for her sin
Of this big omission
Lord, be at her side.

I Beseech Thee Lord

Let me serve Thee with all my heart
Let laziness play no part
For the rest of my days
On earth
Be near me as I utter my words
And do my daily chores
Be they big or small
Give meaning to my life
So I may serve Thee
Forgive my broken promises
Made to Thee in my desperation
Let my life be in Thy shadow
So I may be worthy of Thee
Lord have mercy
Have mercy
On this Thy humble devotee.

My Lord

In silence of the heart
A wish called prayer arises
That each dawn brings new hope
Never again in misery to grope
To walk in Thy shadow
Our only desire is to follow
In the path of Thy glory
In the shade of Thy mercy
Lord hear our prayer
O universal Creator
Lend us Thy ear
Our prayers to hear
In poem and in verse
In the song for the universe
Hold us tight
By the wisdom of Thy light
In the palm of Thy hand
So we may safely land
At Thy door
At death's hour.

My Lord

I am at Thy door
Longing for a glimpse supreme
Of Thy kingdom as of a dream
Lord, accept this sinner
As a daily ringer
Always at Thy door
Begging for more and more
Do I deserve that special grace?
To behold Thy holy face
To be given that special sight
To observe Thy holy might
I do not meditate
Am not in a prayerful state
Yet I long to see Thee
To behold Thy mystery
Lord answer my prayers
Take in hand my affairs
To obey Thy holy writ
To which my life to fit.

I Must Keep Praying

Working or resting
Therein lies my salvation
In it my consolation
That is my only release
As this life flees
At a furious pace
Racing a trivial race
It will not be won
Without help from the ONE
The one and only God
Yours and mine
Our Lord Divine
So keep praying
Working or resting
Till your spirit soars
To the realm of the gods.

I Return to Thee Time and Again

Seeking refuge in Thy domain
Otherworldly it may be
Metaphysical thou may be
In Thee I believe
As Thy creation I perceive
I run to Thee like a lost child
When the world appears hostile
And the pitfalls child like
Then I seek Thee out
And talk to Thee all about
O Lord hear me out
Close not Thy door
Hear my prayer
Help my children's affairs
Help their cares
Help the children of the world
For they are the future of the world.

I Call Thee Krishna

Sometimes Thou art Rama
I call Thee Allah
At times Buddha
Lord Jesus Thou art
Heart of my heart
I worship Thee
With my soul within
With all that I am
I am Thy child I am
Accept me in Thy flock
Thou art my rock
Thou art my all
Have mercy on all
Have mercy, have mercy
On all my calls for when I am lost
My search for Thee goes on
It shall never end
Till for me Thee send.

I Have Come to Pay My Homage

To Thee my Lord and master
I long for Thy grace
My Lord and master
Thou art in my heart
Thou art in my soul
Help me to play my part
To reach Thee, my only goal
I bow to Thy earthly image
In my heartfelt homage
My salvation I seek
To Thee as I pine to reach
So help me God
My omnipresent Lord.

My Lord I Hope

You are there and not
Just my fancy of sorts
For if you are not
Then the world would fall
In one big black hole
And nothing would be anymore
And all our dreams galore
Would end in a furore
And who would we pray to
Whose counsel to take
Who to bow to and scrape
Not another soul
That is for sure.

O Lord Have Mercy

Come live in my heart
Without Thee it is lonely
Have searched Thee near and far
Please come into my home and heart
Have chanted the only mantras
Have read the Scriptures
Have said the prayers as I know
Have failed to reach Thee you know
My world is deserted and empty
Have mercy, have mercy
Thou art my only God
Come live in my soul
Fill the world with Thy grace
And hear as we pray
Without Thee no one is there
Thou, my mantara, my soul
Thou my hymn, my song.

Dear Lord, Thy Servant I Am

Seeking refuge in Thy guidance
Hold my hand and lead Thou me on
Correct me when I am wrong
As a father to a child
As a guardian to a throng
Lead thou on, lead thou on
For our ignorance is blinding
We are lost and wandering
We have lost our purpose
We have lost our insight
Be our eternal guide
That is our prayer
O merciful Father
Heed our endeavour
For Thou art God
The Supreme Lord.

That I Should Love Thee Above All

Is my privilege, O Lord
Thou art that; tvum tat asi
I see Thy infinite glory
In leaf and flower of creation
Here Thou art in the petal of a rose
Or in the melody of a prose
Now in the beauty of the sunset
We recognize Thy holy self
Or to see in the golden dawn
Thy power on eastern horizon
Here I see Thy presence
In the flight of the pheasant
Or the joy in a baby's smile
As it coos and caas a while
Here Thou art
In the beat of the heart
Or a thought in mind's eye
Thou art the supreme reality
Or an illusion it seems
In a dreamer's dream
Thou art knowledge, wisdom
The spirit of the soul
Thou art the king of the soul
The mind, Thy kingdom to rule
Thou art brother, father
Kith and kin, Thou the mother
I bow to Thee in all humility
Begging for Thy mercy.

Heavenly Father

I turn to Thee not for material gain
I turn to Thee on matters of fate
Or to reaffirm my faith
In ups and downs of life to face.
For guidance I turn to Thee
When in sorrow mostly
Or to beg forgiveness
For thoughtlessness
And to Thee I lay bare my soul
And Thou art my very own
For in Thy arms I am reborn
O Lord keep a tight hold
On Thy servant, the lost soul.

Heavenly Father

At Thy shrine are many devotees
They extol Thee in their song
That rises from their soul
They beg for mercy and grace
As they sing their song of praise
They want to reach Thee for sure
As they travel this long road
The night is dark and deep
They are on a mission to seek
Thee till the everlasting sleep
And they will sing till they sleep
That everlasting sleep

Om

I look for Thee from door to door
A pilgrimage to Thy holy shore
From hour to hour
My search grows longer
My desire grows stronger
Now attuned to failure
Where art Thou my Saviour?
Will I ever succeed
Will I ever benediction receive?
Remains to be seen
But the search goes on
The desire is strong
To see Thee face to face
To win my life's race
To fall at Thy feet
To kiss Thy hand
To end my search
Thy shore as I reach
Hold me in Thy sacred grip
Never let me slip
Into unholy ways
At Thy feet to end my days
That is all I have craved
Lord, I beg to be saved.

I Have Come To Thy Shrine

O, my Lord Divine
I lay my burdens at Thy feet
For me there is no other sleep
For I have my word to keep
To Thee my Lord
Before I sleep
The eternal sleep
When finally I shall meet
With Thee my Lord
Face to face
In Thy heavenly abode
On that divine road
Where only the gods dwell
It shall be a time of accountability
It shall be a day of restitution
As I beg for forgiveness
Hoping for kindness
Hoping for a reprieve
Have mercy then my Lord
To fill my beggar's bowl
Have mercy, my Lord.

Heavenly Father

Lend Thy help to the forgotten
The humble and the abandoned
Let there be food on their table
Let their homes be stable
But first a roof over their head
And some jam on their bread
Of racism there be no sign
Make ethnicity colour-blind
Old age erases all differences
As we end mortal existences
Our battles are fought
Some are won and some are lost
Some fought the good fight
Others were overcome by fright
But now it is time to go
Never to return
From that final sojourn.

O Lord Hear My Silent Voice

Thou art my ultimate choice
In Thy holy shrine
I find Thy love divine
It is here that I find solace
By Thy guidance my sins to efface
It is here that I seek refuge
From the worldly subterfuge
For Thou art my reality
Thou art my sacred deity
Who I revere most
Without Thy grace I am lost
O save me from folly
O Thou Lord most holy
Hear my silent voice
Thou art my ultimate choice.

Dear Lord

Admit me in Thy fold
Thou art my silver
Thou art my gold
Thou art my all
Thou art supreme God
My Lord
This is my prayer
Please keep them safe
And make them behave
Kindly to all
O supreme Lord
Be merciful to all
Thy creatures great and small
My Lord please find
A husband kind
For my eldest child
My Lord let all be honest
And follow Thee best
In all they do
In honour and glory too
To Thee my Lord
Have mercy
My Lord have mercy.

Lord of the Universe

I bow to Thee in homage
To touch base with Thee
Is to begin the day rightly
Be our guide today as always
Keep us on the straight and narrow
To work for a happier tomorrow
Where not to hurt all Thy humanity
And never to desecrate its sanctity
Is to be the goal of our testimony
To Thy creative harmony
Lord hear our plea
We bring our faults to Thee
To be forgiven and be guided
On shores of piety to be landed
To be set on the path of virtue
A covenant to be entered into
Thy call to heed, to survive
In all the days of our lives.

Why Do We Pray?

To keep our demons at bay
To find inner peace
When we lay bare
Our heart and soul
In the house of God
When in supplication we kneel
In humility we feel
The presence of God
In our being and in our soul
When we are down in the dumps
And there is nowhere else to turn
We lay bare our pained soul
Before our God
When in dark despair
We search our God
And beg for mercy and courage
To face our hurdles not all alone.

My Lord

My prayers are of the soul
Prayers of one all alone
Some go to the bottle
Some to the needle
I go for the battle
With Thee my Lord
Thou art the heart throb
That turns me on
To the spiritual dawn
Only to Thee I am drawn
When I am down
In the dumps of despair
Sadness is always there
A longing to see Thee
A longing to reach Thee
How steep the path
How long the road
Before I find Thee Lord?

Our Father

Lend us Thine ear
For our prayers to hear
Lead us on righteous ways
Till the end of our days
Make us a world where truth rules
With brotherly love equality rules
A world without hate
No colour or creed
Freed of greed
With justice supreme
Equally treat
All Thy creatures.

Temple in this House of God

I have come to surrender my all
here have I come to seek thee
And to find the secret of Thy mystery
Here in this silence is Thy eternity
It is filled with Thy glory
And with Thy bountiful mercy
Here will I find the peace
Here perchance Thy grace
Here will I beg with a beggar's bowl
For Thy mercy for all
Here in the silence of the house of God
In the adoration of the Song
Will I find the heart of Thy soul
And reach Thee to become whole.

In Praise of Thee

O Lord, let my life be devoted to Thy service
O Lord, lead me on the path of righteousness
So I may be worthy to behold Thy glory
In its splendour and mystery
O my friend, lead me to Thy abode
Where dwell only the gods
So I may witness Thy holy splendour
And to Thee my service render
Lead me from the unreal to the real
From darkness to light
From death to immortality
O Lord have mercy, have mercy
On this Thy servant, on this Thy devotee
O Lord, lead me in Thy footsteps
Let me dwell on Thy holy doorsteps.

My Lord Nirvana

I am longing for Thee
To be one with Thee
That is all I want
That is all I crave
I have a desire to behold
Thy magnificence bright as gold
O Master of the world
In Thy palm Thou me hold
And never let me go
O Master, O Creator
Do not desert me now
I am a lost soul
Keep me in Thy fold
Keep tight Thy hold
And never let me go
From under Thy shadow
Never let me slip
From under Thy grip
Hold me tight
Under Thy wings to hide.

My Lord

I am back at Thy door
Please open Thy heart
To my helpless plight
And help me to rise
From the doldrums of life
Not to keep sinking
Deeper, darker thinking
Doing absolutely nothing
Just to die waiting
Please help me, Lord
Help, my dear Lord
With vigour and energy
So I can always keep working
In Thy shadow
In the glow of Thy halo
Please, Lord, make me worthy
Of this life's journey
So when death claims me finally
With no regrets it shall be.

Om

To the glory of God
I give my salute
To His haven I have returned
After a time in wilderness
Where only cynicism grows
Where only naysayers thrive
I must believe in the universal Creator
Of compassion and mercy
Of love and charity
Where humans live in harmony
Where the strong help the weak
Where love conquers all
O Lord, in that haven of freedom
Let this sinner arrive
To help those who need it the most.

Om

Without Thy help I cannot proceed
Without Thy guidance I cannot meet
The burden of my duties
My Lord, I have returned to Thee
After the wilderness of unbelief
Thy grace I seek
Thy advice to heed
Take me under Thy wing
Hold me in a tight grip
Let me not slip
Into darkness of sloth and slumber
O life, O keep me
Secure in the palm of Thy hand
My Lord, a sinner knocketh at Thy door
Looking for comfort and hope
Turn me not away
To roast in some hell once again
I beg Thy pardon
For all my shortcomings
Hold me close
As I weep at Thy door
In Thy faith
Is my everlasting stake
Guide me, O Lord
Never to be lazy at all.

Om

There comes a moment
When you are helpless
Not knowing which way to turn
When you hurt and hurt
Hoping for some help
From the Lord perhaps
But you wait and wait
With your sadness and pain
Your hurt and no grace
Yet you must face
Each fresh day
Is like any
No forays ever help
No other help
Except from above perhaps.

O Lord

Where art Thou?
That Thou art
Of that there is no doubt
But a mystery doth shroud
Of Thy whereabouts
Some say Thou art omnipresent
Some call Thee nature resplendent
That Thou art in every soul
That Thou maketh us whole
Of that there is no doubt
With Thy mystery Thou us surround
But to some Thou art an unknown
The agnostics and atheists
Know Thee not in their soul
Unto themselves they are gods
These self-confident egoists
Deride the believers
That Thou art our keeper
And we Thy reapers
So have mercy on us all
Thy children we are all.

O Lord

Give me patience and fortitude
I bow to Thee in gratitude
Lead me on to the high road
Guide me to lofty goals
Give me the will to carry them through
Lead me not to waste time
Let me seek and find
The best in human mind
Let me be Thy disciple, O Lord
Come what may, O Lord
Let Thy light so shine
On me and mine
And on the world beside
That we walk in Thy shadow
On all the days of our lives
Lord, keep us under Thy care
That is my prayer
O Lord, I hop Thou does hear
The voice of this nobody
Who is Thy ardent devotee.

O Lord, I Come to Thy Shrine

After a long time
I get waylaid at the roadside
And forget my duties by Thy side
I am lazy and shirk my duty
And let the time pass by
Hence my life has been a waste
Rationalizing all sins of omission
Finding excuses to avoid my mission
Of helping the sick and hungry
I have grown into a replica of a failure
Hiding behind the cloak of aging
I could have done more
With my life for sure
Such is my sadness and sorrow
At wasted life that harrows.

O Lord

Forgive me, O Lord
If you find it in your heart
To give me a new start
Then pardon me, Lord
For wasting my life away
Dozing off on a recliner
At eventide after supper
If I count the number of hours
They multiply into many years
And this, my Lord, is the measure
Of not success but failures
It is like numbing the brain
So it may feel no pain
It is like shutting the eye
From an empty life
To building a cocoon around
So none may ever hound
This coward of a person
That I have turned into
Have mercy, my Lord
On sinners like me, O Lord.

Om

Be my inspiration, Lord
Carry me through
I have lost my way
Dark is my day
I let moments slip by
Resting, always waiting
I fail to find my way
Help me across
From this morass
I am a lost soul
Amidst the lost throng
Like some lost sheep
We are tossed from heap to heap
No shepherd to guide
Nowhere to hide
Our loneliness and sorrow
Counting our days to the morrow
When we shall meet Thee
At last on that final journey
Hear our cry, Lord
In this world we are lost
Help us, Lord
We are the lost souls.

A Prayer of Adoration

Thou, Lord of Creation
I long to see Thee face to face
I long to receive Thy grace
Thou who created such beauty
Are the supreme architect heavenly
I bow to Thee, I praise Thee
In all Thy omniscient glory
I see Thee in the petal of a rose
And hear Thee in a bird song
Or in the thunder and lightening
When in anger Thou are chiding
I see Thy glory in the setting sun
When the sky is painted a copper tone
Above all, I beg Thee for many a favour
Hoping that Thou art there
To hear my song of prayer
That begs and implores
That praises and adores
That asks for more and more
That hopes and hopes
That one day I shall see Thee
In all Thy resplendent glory
Then I shall fall at Thy feet
And beg to become one with Thee
And achieve Nirvana through piety.

As I Sit of an Evening

Alone, without company
My thoughts fly to Thee
My Lord Supreme
Then I meditate, seeing Thee
In my mind's eye
I see Thee in all Thy glory
Now still, now smiling
All my loneliness is flown
Am no longer alone
For I have Thee
In my mind's eye
I have Thee in my heart
Never to be apart
Engulfed in Thy mystery
Bathed in Thy effulgence
Comforted in Thy presence
And this I pray
May this spell never fray
Lord have mercy
Till my life's eternity.

Love, Hope and Charity

Come before mercy
Without love
You cannot forgive
Without hope
You cannot cope
Without charity
You lack spirituality
For all of the above
To God give thy love
Through silent prayer
For the grace to bear
Any burden, any hardship
To do Lord's will as worship.

Prayer

O touch me with Thy mercy
O touch me with Thy grace
O let me witness Thy glory
At a favoured range
O let me behold
Thy creation new and old
Where only the gods reside
The mystery to hide
O let me deserve
All that I ask for
Let me be at Thy feet
Come like some lost sheep
Let me be at Thy feet
For an everlasting sleep
No more to wander and weep
O touch me with that grace
Which shows me Thy holy face.

This is My Daily Prayer

My Lord be nearer, be nearer
My longing to behold Thee
Face to face in Thy company
Is all I desire and live for
I have been a wanderer before
But now hold me tight
In Thy glory bright
And never let me go
My lord, never let me go
This I beseech
When will I reach
That height divine
Where only the chosen find
That divine grace
When they see Thee face to face

My Lord God

I am back at Thy abode
With joined hands and bowed head
In supplication I tread
This path to Thy holy shrine
To drink deep at Thy spiritual mine
I have a heart full of devotion
Full of longing emotion
That I may see Thee face to face
To be showered by Thy special grace
O Lord, find a husband for my love one
Find a partner for my cherished one.

The Golden Dawn is Bright

And I am at Thy shrine
To pay my homage at Thy abode
In my heart I Thee adore
Beside Thee there is no other god
For at this holy place
All who come to pray
For a moment's peaceful sway
And lay down their woes
At Thy doors
For at Thy feet
I find my peace
In my mind Thou abide
In my soul Thou do reside
And Thou art at my side
On my life's lonely ride.

Thank You, Lord

For all the small mercies
Whether deserved or not
Thank you, dear Lord
How often I fail to see
That my begging bowl
Is only half empty
Thank you, Lord, for this day
Its bright morning ray
Is the cure of a prayer
Thank you for all Thy bounty
From Thee my God Almighty.

Work is My Salvation

O Lord, keep me busy
In doing my rightful duty
So I may forever be busy
In doing some charity
In a state of piety
My Lord hold us tight
In the palm of Thy hand
And let our lives be not lost
Who are suffering most
And need Thy helping hand
O our eternal Lord.

My Prayers to God

Reach not the Lord
Thou art my all
O my gracious Lord
Take my hand
Help me to stand
Firmly on Thy holy land
O Lord my soul
Keep me in Thy fold
I await Thy call
Enshrining Thee in my soul
Awaiting Thy call
For Thou art my all.

My Lord

Who comes to you more
Than I do
Who complains more
Than I do
Who needs you more
Than I do
Who dialogues with you
More than I do
Who sends all these notes
More than I do
Who is lazier than I am
Who is a bigger beggar
Than I am
Who disobeys you more
Than I do
Hence I am a weaker soul
Do not give up on me, Lord
Keep me on your roll
Therefore forgiveness
Is what I need
So I may pay heed
To Thy rules
To learn in Thy school
To stop being a fool
And obey Thy rules.

My Lord

Tell the truth
Says our Lord God
Be honest
Says the conscience
Be good
Love all
Do not lie
Not to You
Nor to anyone
Follow the Lord
Waste not your life
Do good
Alleviate suffering
Expect no rewards
For the good you do
Pray for strength
To do the right thing
In spite of fears
Have faith
Faith will give courage
Follow thy God
For he will save thy soul
Have no fear
For to God
You are very dear.

My Lord, My Lord

Where art thou?
My longing to see Thee
Is getting the better of me
My Lord have mercy
On this Thy servant
Who is a straw in the wind
Buffeted by Nature's whim
Have mercy
Show me the way
Lead me on
To the sanctuary of Thy abode
Show me the way
My Lord, have mercy.

My Prayers Have No Power

My prayers are just wishes
My wishes do not come true
There is nothing I can do
But I must keep praying
Must not go a-straying
Without self-help
An empty hand is dealt
The prayers have no yield
It is harvesting an empty field
Keep working towards your goal
On your lips keep the name GOD
One day your prayers shall be heard
And the Lord will keep His word.

Lord

I bow to Thee in supplication
I am Thy servant at Thy feet
Lead me by the hand
To Thy pastures green
On the path that is righteous
That I may follow in obedience
To Thy great commandments
Lord, light up Thy lamp
In my children's path
That they may walk in Thy step
Lord, favour Gita's fate
That she may husband take
If Thou so wills it
Then let it be true
I bow and beg Thee
I am Thy humble devotee
That I may always do good
By all creatures great and small.

Lord as the Golf Pro

The Lord is a golf pro
His balls are the planets
His links span the outer space
His cup is deep as black holes
His putt reaches the orbits
His green is the universe
His drive is speedy as a shooting star
We the mortals are his caddies
Eagle, birdie, hole in one
Are his marks of a champion
He is the master golfer
His game has the world astir
On a more serious note
He is also a master scientist
Whose mystery is unsolvable
But we sure shall keep trying
Till the secret answer we find.

The Skies Are Blue

The earth is shrouded in garbs of pristine snow
The frozen Credit River can no longer flow
The maples tall and stately but bared of leaf
The solitary robin takes a peek
At the squirrel hastening past
In search of an acorn at last
All this panorama is Thy shrine
All the birdsong a prayerful rhyme
And a prayer rises from the heart
Lord, let no man tear apart
This Thy shrine in wonderland
Created by Thy masterful hand
For a man to wonder and pray
At Thy masterful array
And still the wonder may grow
How to reach Thee somehow?

In My Meditations

When I lay bare my soul
At Thy temple abode
The peace therein is filled
With silence sublime
I am filled with a longing
To behold Thy earthly face
Lo! I see Thy majesty all around me
I see Thee in the glow of the golden dawn
In the light of the setting sun
I hear Thee in the flight of the early bird
Making music as it explores the blue skies
I see Thy mystery in the petals of a rose
And its essence in the scent past my nose
I feel Thee in the gentle caress
Of the breeze brushing past my cheek
It is Thy spirit that I espy all around me
Thy spirit in motion all about me
It is Thee that Thou art
That Thou art Thou art.

Shape Our Affairs

For the Lord cares
For our affairs
He shapes our destiny
With His infinite mercy
He guides us
He provides us
So to Him look up
With all Thy might
Through all the strife
He is the guide
His is the life
That runs through mine.

My Prayers Are of Supplication

Often of adoration
Some born of desperation
With strong faith
Your prayers cannot fail
To be answered
But you must try your best
To work without rest
To achieve your goal
With the help of the Lord
Hard work and prayers
Go hand in hand
One without the other—a futile gesture
For prayer without work
May not get fulfilled.

At Thy Holy Door I Sing

All longings I bring
And I pray and pray
And I say my say
Know I now
I may bow and bow
But having failed to do my duty
Undeserved my gratuity
Nothing is for free
If from your duty you flee
Miracles do not happen I hear
To hard work if you are not geared
Prayer and work go hand in hand
Life slips by if you stand and stand
Miracles happen only to those
Hard work who chose.

Rises From the Depth of My Soul

That Thy temple be in my home
That I behold Thee face to face
That Thy realm be my base
That I continue my search
At last find Thee and reach
Thy holy abode where the gods reside
To be forever at Thy side
Doing Thy bidding awake or asleep
Even seeing Thee in my dreams
Yet how far I am from Thee now
How many lifetimes it will be
To reach Thee somehow!

O Creator of this universe
Where dost Thou hide
In the creation is Thy majesty
This panorama is Thy artistry
This world is Thy miracle
Thy omnipresence its pinnacle
And we who want to unravel Thy mystery
Know all about its difficulty
So guide us anon
With a whimper and a song
So we may reach Thee
Maybe, maybe.

O Lord, Your Kindly Light

Lead Thou us on
The life is idle
And I am not in the saddle
Each day slips by
And I never try
To walk in Thy footsteps
All I do is rest and rest
And never try my best.
Lend me Thy hand of grace
Spur my mind to face
The realities of life
And do my best to fight
This fit of lethargy
That has changed me into an effigy
Of indolent do-nothing
Who expects hand-me-outs
Without lifting a finger
To change for the better
O lift me from this morass
And lead me to the high mass
Lead Thou me on
O kindly light anon.

To Pine For God at All Times

To pine with the pain of a lover
To have the burning desire to see Him
To have the urge to have dialogue with Him
To see Him face to face in all His glory
In all His resplendent mystery
To behold Him is all I want
And yet the Gita tells us that to behold Him
One needs divine vision
That only the gods possess
Leaving all desires behind
Conquering ambition for wealth and power
Overcoming fear, anger, jealously and lust
Renouncing worldly joys, pleasures
Aiming only at a higher purpose
Of service performed unselfishly
For the good of one and all.

My Wishes Are Many

My requests are a-plenty
Like a mendicant I am at Thy door
Asking for more and more
Thou hast many like me
Always begging and always hungry
Thou asks and rightly so
Why don't you work towards your goal
Instead of asking for more and more
But my Lord I have tried and failed
So I turn to Thee again and again
And some things are not in my hands to get
Some things are not at my reach
So I turn to Thee and beseech
And try to get Thee to heed
And I shall keep trying till you heed.

I Pray For Benediction

I pray for heavenly grace
For a world without hate
And one without misery
That no one should go hungry
That there is shelter for all
And all children go to school
Compulsory education the rule
With kindness to treat each other
As a sister or a brother
And share our largesse
With those who are blessed with less
And help each other
As a brother to a brother
And we pray that the skies stay blue
And oceans not overflow
And our fields stay green
Our lakes abundant with fish
And in friendship we live
And the earth beneath our feet
Does not spew earthquake heat
And cast, colour and creed
Becomes ancient history
O to live in a world without hate
Should be our everlasting fate.

In Praise of Thee

Thou art the universal father
Thy seat is every being's soul
Thou art omnipresent for all
Thou readeth our thoughts
Thou knoweth our wishes
Teach us to be true to Thee
And of dogma to be free
And by self-realisation to see Thee
In our life works daily
Free us of hypocrisy
To be true to Thee
In all our dealing
To live in praise of Thee
And crave for Thy mercy
This is our prayer
This is our supplication
To always be true to Thee
In our mind's eye.

Thou Art So Far Away

Thou hath helped me always
Now I seek Thee again
For relief of my inner pain
Tell me the ways that I may
Reach Thee in the end
My Lord, fill my empty abode
With Thy presence once more
O Lord, why hath thou deserted me?
Where art thou, hear me
O Creator and myth maker
Lend me Thy hand
Hold me near to Thy heart
O Lord, desert me not
When I need Thee the most.

Lord, Forgive Me My Sins

Lord, let not these sins
Come upon my children
Let the punishment be mine
As I beg forgiveness Thine
Lead me on the right road
Hold my hand, Lord
For I am lost
Save my soul
My Lord have mercy
On persons each and every
We week Thy grace
We seek Thy guidance
For Thou art the father
Thou the mother
Thou the saviour
Thou the redeemer
In Thee we rest our faith
As we seek Thy grace
Amen.

My Lord of the Heavens Above

Steer me away from selfishness
Lead me to the realms of self-sacrifice
Let me be the seeker after truth
Abolish the sin of indolence in me
This I pray my Lord
Let me do my best for all
Let me be the helper
Let me be the giver
And not a perpetual taker
Not a mere sitter but a doer
Above all let me waste not my life
As old age hastens my time
Lord have mercy on this lost soul
Forgive me my sins and all.

O Heavenly Father

Keep me away from evil
Let my thoughts be of ideals
Lead me away from temptation
My heart full of compassion
To serve Thee my passion
To live under Thy guidance
Bless us Thy children
And keep us from harm's way
By the sweat of our labour
Let our harvests be full
Thy commandments our rule
Scriptures our word.

I Weave Garlands of Marigolds

Thy holy form to adorn
I gather fresh flowers in the morn
Thine shrine to adorn
I compose the welcome song
To play on the harpsichord
When Thy visible form I behold
When will that be, my Lord?
O please give me Thy word
That one day I shall see Thee
Face to face in all Thy glory
Thy face is the face of truth
Consolation to those that hurt
Human kindliness Thy glory
Child's innocence Thy purity
Thy soul the soul of true devotee
How will I know Thee
When Thee revisit this planet?
As a Christ perchance?
Will Thee give a sign in advance?
O Lord I long to be
With Thee in all Thy mercy.

Look at the Bright Side

At the dawn of each day
At the end of the day
Count your blessings
In these life lessons
You have done your duty
To live by the rule book of decency
If you have then life will go easy
And if you have not
Then your conscience
Will not let you sleep for an instant
You will toss and turn and wonder
What went wrong
At the trouble you wrought
The fear of getting caught
Will make your innards turn
Pray that you pass your days in honesty
For this a priceless virtue in all truth
Keep your conscience clear
No matter what you do
Truth be your only God
Duty be your only road
Guided by the Lord.

Let There Be Heaven on Earth

Instead of poverty and curse
Freed of hunger and want
Where the virtuous take a stand
Where basic humanity is the rule
And loving kindness the goal
Where there are fields of ripening wheat
And food in abundant heaps
No pollution of crystal clear lakes
Blossoming hillsides never to desecrate
Where there is laughter and cheer
Instead of cruelty and fear
Where the mountains ring with prayer
In praise of the gods that are there
O Lord let all be happy
And all are full of humanity.

Let Such Verse in my Soul Abound

The equal of which is not found
Let its melody rise from the soul
For the benefit of one and all
Let me to the world expound
How in love to Thee I am bound
Let the song in praise of Thee
Be on every lip universally
My Lord fill me with Thy holy grace
So I may sing those songs of praise
My love of Thee is one of longing
To realize Thee in my being
So Ye may so reside in my soul
With Thee to become one whole
This is my prayer
This is my chant
This is all I want.

In Praise of Thee

Thou art the Creator
The mystery maker
Thou art the father
The all-embracing mother
Thou art Guru Brahma
Guru Vishnu, Guru Deva
Thou art Mahashvara
Thou art omnipresent
Thou art omniscient
Thou art wisdom
Thou art knowledge
Thou art my all
Thou art my everlasting God!

Books by Saroj Daulat Ram:

• *Songs of Praise based on the Bhagavad Gita*
2011

• *A Tribute to Gandhiji in verse*
2011

• *Tulsi Ramayan*
2013

• *Daily Prayer Lifelines*
2013

Books available through the author.

www.ingramcontent.com/pod-product-compliance
Lightning Source LLC
Chambersburg PA
CBHW052114110526
44592CB00013B/1609